1,000,000 Books

are available to read at

Forgotten Books

www.ForgottenBooks.com

Read online
Download PDF
Purchase in print

ISBN 978-0-243-48618-2
PIBN 10800155

This book is a reproduction of an important historical work. Forgotten Books uses state-of-the-art technology to digitally reconstruct the work, preserving the original format whilst repairing imperfections present in the aged copy. In rare cases, an imperfection in the original, such as a blemish or missing page, may be replicated in our edition. We do, however, repair the vast majority of imperfections successfully; any imperfections that remain are intentionally left to preserve the state of such historical works.

Forgotten Books is a registered trademark of FB &c Ltd.
Copyright © 2018 FB &c Ltd.
FB &c Ltd, Dalton House, 60 Windsor Avenue, London, SW19 2RR.
Company number 08720141. Registered in England and Wales.

For support please visit www.forgottenbooks.com

1 MONTH OF FREE READING

at

www.ForgottenBooks.com

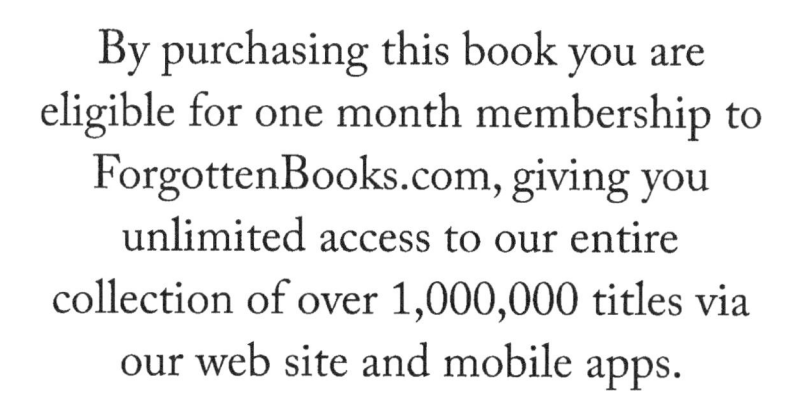

By purchasing this book you are eligible for one month membership to ForgottenBooks.com, giving you unlimited access to our entire collection of over 1,000,000 titles via our web site and mobile apps.

To claim your free month visit：

www.forgottenbooks.com/free800155

* Offer is valid for 45 days from date of purchase. Terms and conditions apply.

English
Français
Deutsche
Italiano
Español
Português

www.forgottenbooks.com

Mythology Photography **Fiction**
Fishing Christianity **Art** Cooking
Essays Buddhism Freemasonry
Medicine **Biology** Music **Ancient Egypt** Evolution Carpentry Physics
Dance Geology **Mathematics** Fitness
Shakespeare **Folklore** Yoga Marketing
Confidence Immortality Biographies
Poetry **Psychology** Witchcraft
Electronics Chemistry History **Law**
Accounting **Philosophy** Anthropology
Alchemy Drama Quantum Mechanics
Atheism Sexual Health **Ancient History**
Entrepreneurship Languages Sport
Paleontology Needlework Islam
Metaphysics Investment Archaeology
Parenting Statistics Criminology
Motivational

TEACHING THE PEOPLE'S LANGUAGE

by

PAUL WITTY
School of Education, Northwestern University

and

LOU LaBRANT
School of Education, New York University

*Prepared for the Service Center of the
American Education Fellowship*

HINDS, HAYDEN & ELDREDGE, Inc.
NEW YORK   PHILADELPHIA

CONTENTS

		Page
I	THE PROBLEM	1
II	HOW LANGUAGE GROWS	10
III	CONCLUSION — ENDS AND MEANS	29
	SUGGESTED READINGS	33

COPYRIGHT, 1946, BY

HINDS, HAYDEN & ELDREDGE, INC.

PRINTED IN THE UNITED STATES OF AMERICA

THE PROBLEM

There are times when it is appropriate for teachers to consider the niceties of presenting some subject, or to discuss the preferred method for developing specific skills. But there are other occasions when primary thought should be given to problems of paramount significance, and immediate action should follow. The writers believe that the teaching of the English language in the schools of the United States is a large and critical issue *now*. Even a cursory consideration of the significant role language plays in achieving an understanding and appreciation of postwar problems makes this fact apparent.

Our century has seen the dramatic development of the radio as a means of communication; within a very few hours it is now possible for announcements to be heard by millions of individuals throughout the world. At the same time this expansion was taking place, there were also some unparalleled examples of restriction in communication. Thus, one strong nation refused its people free access to the radio and denied them the right to read, hear, or discuss the truth. Germany's blackout of the news was accompanied by a gross exploitation of language. Words were used to stir emotion; statements were made with open disregard for facts; books were burned; and listening to the foreign radio was prohibited. When language is thus abused, disintegration and chaos surely follow.

As Lewis Mumford states in *Faith for Living*:

> In short, man's greatest triumph in producing order out of chaos, greater than law, greater than science, was language. To keep the channels of human communication clean is a duty as primal — and holy — as

guarding the sacred fire was for primitive man. He who debases the word as the fascists have so unsparingly done, breeds darkness and confusion and all manner of foulness.

It is difficult to discuss changes in language without appearing to repeat generalizations which already have grown trite. Nevertheless, we urge the teacher of English to consider the following facts which have altered the role of language in the world today.

Increase in reading has accompanied technological development. The radio and moving-talking picture are not the only developments which have influenced language. The last decade has seen the rise of inexpensive books and of special issue magazines which serve the purpose of books. The popular paperbound twenty-five cent book is now produced by a dozen or more companies; it reaches a public largely untouched by the expensive cloth-bound book. Among these cheap books there are some rather inferior volumes, but there are also great books as well as an increasing number of what Ruskin called "good books of the hour." The sale in hundreds of thousands of a popularly priced edition of Wendell Wilkie's *One World* is illustrative of the new demand for serious discussions of contemporary social problems.

During World War II, our men in the armed forces read a great many books and magazines. In the first days of the war they read many technical books, and volumes dealing with the war and its progress. Later on, they preferred, among nonfiction titles, books on postwar planning, and discussions of personal problems. But they were also reading many novels and biographies. According to a report by Chaplain E. C. Nance in *Publishers' Weekly* (February 17, 1945) there were more than 2,000 competently staffed Army libraries in which more than 15,000,000 books were available. The Navy had more than 5,000 libraries, on ship and shore; and every Army division going overseas took with it a library of 8,000 books. Analyses of circulation figures are revealing: for example, the librarian in Fort Monmouth reports that the 38,000 volumes in the various libraries on this post were read on the average three times during a twelve month period. Seven non-fiction books were read to every five books of straight fiction. The relative popularity of fiction and non-fiction titles varies of course, but one inescapable fact is brought out in these studies: our Army was a reading Army. Moreover, the majority of selections were relatively high in quality. Some of the books most in demand in Fort Devens, from January to June, 1944, were: *A Tree Grows in Brooklyn, Undercover, Here Is Your War, D Day, The Razor's Edge, While Still We Live, Strange Woman, A Bell for Adano, Helmets and Lipstick, Brave Men*, and *Thirty Seconds over Tokyo*. More than 900,000 men enrolled in the United States Armed Forces Institute, taking 500 different courses in 20 fields of study. This demand for study courses necessitated the printing of 15,000,000 textbooks.

Civilian reading has also changed. Librarians are reporting that civilians are again coming to libraries frequently; during the first two years of war, attendance dropped; it has again been resumed.

Civilians are buying books more frequently than before, including such inexpensive volumes as the Pocket Books, Penguin, Pelican, and other popular editions. This development may have wide influence on the reading habits of our people. Today, for ten or twenty dollars, it is possible to purchase a rather comprehensive library, as a number of lists compiled from twenty-five cent offerings show. Sale of such a book as *Here Is Your War* by Ernie Pyle in an expensive format, without detracting from its simultaneous sale as a Pocket Book, indicates that a reading audience long limited by lack of money is being served. What this may mean to the next generation is incalculable. For the present, these new demands and interests in reading cannot fail to affect the curriculum of the secondary school and college.

The literate adult is using the radio to secure information which he once obtained from the press. It is probable that the public is now better informed on national and world affairs as a result of listening to news and comment on the radio than a similar population was in 1920, when dependence for news was placed on newspapers and magazines. The radio makes it possible to acquire, in a comparatively short time, information which could be obtained only through many hours of careful reading of several newspapers. Moreover, the individual now hears different points of view, as well as expert comment comparable to that found in editorials. It is clear that teachers of English should be quite as much concerned with teaching students how to select and listen to radio programs as with teaching them how to read newspapers critically.

Reading instruction has been complicated further by the fact that listening to the radio has become for many children a substitute for leisure reading. With a minimum of effort, they hear stories of adventure, form associations with groups of characters, and enjoy other exciting experiences. In many programs, the story is presented rapidly, and sound effects replace descriptive paragraphs. Not long ago in the history of civilization, story telling was a major device for imparting information and providing entertainment. Reading books then became a substitute for story telling or listening to stories. In a sense, we are returning to the age of story telling via the radio. What effect this change will have on how children are taught to read is an open question. But it is apparent that the teacher who wishes to interest boys and girls in stories of literary excellence must take into account the fact that pupils can obtain excitement and adventure almost without effort through listening to the radio.

The widening of communication through the radio and other channels has possibilities for good or for bad. The fact that the President brings many issues directly to the people over the radio is illustrative of a new and important problem teachers of English face. As yet we have, in far too many classrooms, treated radio programs as outcasts; or, at best, as devices for stimulating and enriching reading. We must now recognize the fact that listening is a skill which needs to be cultivated and directed.

Stepped up by the war is the use of radio broadcasting by the ordinary citizen. Men who seldom wrote anything but letters or postcards, and read little beyond the local papers, have broadcast their experiences and impressions; they have frequently spoken with simplicity and effectiveness. Private Smith, who tells of his fight on a South Sea island, is making a vast change in his own use of language. High school students who conduct forums on the air are also modifying their language patterns. More and more, men and women and boys and girls are using language in terms of a new set of relations; they are now taking part in an enlarged community of new activities and experiences.

In at least three important areas, the written or spoken word is combined with visual materials in a manner which would have been unbelievable to a citizen of the nineteenth century. These three developments are: the talking picture; the illustrated article where, as in *Life Magazine,* pictures often outweigh script in quantity; and a great variety of narratives and explanations where the comic or cartoon technique is used. One has only to compare the effect of the atrocity pictures which came out of German-occupied countries with the effect of similar verbal accounts to appreciate the power of the picture. It would be strange indeed if children, accustomed to these varied and appealing forms of presentation, did not change their attitudes toward books.

The people's drama has become, in the past twenty years, chiefly the drama of motion pictures and radio. Boys and girls attend movies frequently and rate this medium above the radio in their leisure preferences. Although the average attendance is about once each week, there are some boys and girls who attend the movies three or four times as often. Children like the same elements in the movie that attract them over the radio — action, adventure, excitement, and continuity. The influence of the movies, like that of the radio, is of course neither good nor bad. On the whole, going to movies tends to crystallize existing patterns of thought and to keep thinking on a plateau by repeating the same formula or reinforcing the same idea (as in serial stories). It is doubtful, however, whether growth in taste would occur in reading if there were no more help than is generally given children in the appreciation of radio and movie programs.

Whatever the developments of the radio, the movie, and television may be, teachers must see that teaching drama to persons who see and enjoy a movie each week, and who listen to the radio two hours or more daily, is different from teaching (as in 1920) drama to students who seldom saw or listened to a play of any kind. Once more we encounter the problem of cultivating critical judgment and appreciation with full awareness of the effect of forces operating outside the school.

The comic strip furnishes a new device for communicating. The comics, like the radio and the movie, have almost universal appeal and attract readers in every rank of literacy. According to one study, youngsters in Grades IV to VI read an average of four comic books regularly, and four and one-half others, often. Even in high school, the comic magazines constituted about one-fourth of the total number of magazines read.

It has been observed frequently that adults also read and enjoy the comics. Accordingly, the comic and cartoon techniques are beginning to be recognized as remarkably clear, attractive methods of presenting certain types of subject-matter. The Army has used the comics extensively. For example, in Special Training Units, a magazine is distributed monthly; it contains a comic strip recounting the adventures of Private Pete and Daffy. The men in these units have been repeatedly questioned about their attitude toward this strip. They report that it is their favorite part of the magazine. Organizations which are attempting to present facts about racial and cultural questions are finding the comic or cartoon technique effective, and advertisers make frequent use of it. The speed and ease with which one gains a point or gets the main idea of a story from the comic strip not only suggest its advantages but also account for a changed attitude toward conventional reading material which we find in many readers, young and old.

A new and increased understanding of the nature of language itself is already changing language instruction. One of the major interests of psychologists during the past thirty years has centered in the effect of language upon the individual's development and adjustment. New and important findings have to some extent affected our methods of teaching; we now give more attention to the need of the child for free expression through language; we are more concerned with the role of interest; we give greater attention to interpretation and critical reading; and we are beginning to appreciate the intimate relationship of language expression to mental health.

Despite these gains, there is a regrettable lag between the knowledge of desirable practices and their widespread utilization. Many teachers still appear to believe that students who can pass certain standardized tests are qualified to read critically and with understanding. Yet these tests deal chiefly with the ability of an individual to repeat the contents of a paragraph or a page. We have few tests which seek to discover whether persons can distinguish between significant and insignificant facts. Roma Gans has shown that elementary school pupils may make satisfactory scores on standard tests and still be unable to differentiate relevant from irrelevant facts in passages of supposedly comprehended material. Many children can, it appears, tell what the book says; but they cannot judge either the importance or the pertinence of what is said. Even more significant is a recent study by Sylvia Kay, who reports that many high school seniors are unable to distinguish relevant from irrelevant facts, and to differentiate diametrically opposed conclusions presented in treatments of social issues.

Teachers, as well as all other citizens, should be vitally interested in the fact that the Army was forced to teach many soldiers to read and write. It appears that we are not the literate people we thought ourselves to be. Nevertheless, we have been deciding national and international questions on the assumption that practically all our citizens are capable of making judgments on what the press presents. If we consider the 13 per cent who are functionally illiterate and the additional number who read blindly, we should be amazed that our country has been able to function effectively as a democracy.

The basic reading skills which are developed during the first few years of school are clearly inadequate to meet present-day demands for more complex reading abilities. A program of English which concentrates on the elimination of errors in usage and punctuation, without regard for radio and motion-picture messages and for accounts in daily papers, is as futile as King Canute's orders in the face of the tide. The teaching of reading and of English must aim to improve and foster communication and must make effective use of the varied means through which communication takes place.

Who is to be responsible if we are to have a language program in America commensurate with our opportunity and our necessity? The National Council of Teachers of English has stoutly emphasized discussion of controversial questions, wide reading, introduction to international literature, teaching in terms of individual differences, and study of the nature of language. Despite this effort, there is an overwhelming amount of teaching today which is far removed from the needs we have described, and which, by a false emphasis, is actually harmful. The following suggestions are advanced by the writers as practical steps in carrying forward a program to improve language instruction.

1. *Parents* can make an important contribution. They can cease expecting that only the few items they remember from their own school experience be taught, and they can stop estimating their children's progress solely by their ability to parse, or diagram, or spell. Instead they should ask: Is my child writing and speaking accurately — in terms of his experience? Does he read widely and critically? Can he present simply and clearly

the facts he knows? Does he speak honestly, and feel an obligation to justify what he says? Does he talk without self-consciousness with pupils from other social, racial, and economic groups? Can he exchange ideas without rancor; and as a result of discussion, is he able to modify his opinions? If the parent will place his emphasis upon language as a way of dealing with important problems, he will do much to foster language development.

2. *Teachers in areas other than English* can give essential help. They can recognize their responsibility for teaching English as well as the other subject fields. They also can accept as their criterion of good English ability which includes far more than correct usage, spelling, and punctuation. They, too, can emphasize critical reading and clear communication. Mathematics, history, sociology, and science offer almost unlimited opportunities for stressing critical reading and for examining basic assumptions. Similarly, in other subject areas, these outcomes should be given primary consideration.

3. *School administrators and supervisors* can help by developing comprehensive language programs which are adequate in terms of today's varied school population and the knowledge of language development which we now have. They can assist teachers of English by helping them work out a curriculum which is rooted in a concern for improving and clarifying communication. A principal or superintendent might well, for example, devote a series of faculty and parent meetings to a study of such a book as Hayakawa's *Language in Action,* asking teachers from various areas to present applications of the principles to their particular fields of instruction. An attack as comprehensive as the one recently undertaken by the Writers' War Board* in its work on one phase of language would yield rich returns.

4. *Teachers of English at every level* would profit from a renewed study of language. Such study should lead them:

---

* Writers' War Board, "The Myth That Threatens America," 122 East 42nd St., New York 17, N. Y.

a. To encourage the growth of language for the primary purpose of improving communication. This implies the teaching of reading and other language skills through a meaningful program that is rooted in the experiences and needs of the child.

b. To encourage free communication between individuals in the school; and to make greater and more extensive use of various forms of oral and written expression.

c. To encourage a critical use of language. A concern for critical reading should be one of the primary objectives of instruction in the elementary grades and should continue to be a primary concern at all later periods. Experiences in critical reading should be associated with activities which call for critical evaluation of spoken and written expression.

d. To inform the student concerning the role of language in his own life and in the world scene. Reading, like speaking and writing, should help the pupil understand himself and his social environment.

e. To provide frequent opportunities for talking over controversial issues and for discussing topics of national importance.

f. To develop skill in using or interpreting the varied modern means for communicating — writing, person-to-person conversation, radio, talking pictures, and so forth.

g. To encourage a reading program which is individually purposeful and fully adapted to the wide range of abilities found within every class.

In the following chapter we shall attempt to show how some of these outcomes can be secured.

II

HOW LANGUAGE GROWS

A. Vocabulary

Although it is not the purpose of this pamphlet to describe in detail how a program of language suited to the needs of our present world should be worked out, there is included a brief description of how language grows and of how free expression may be stimulated and guided. That there is confusion concerning this important problem is indicated by the variations in the treatment of units on vocabulary building in textbooks and curricula. These units purport to do many things; some are designed to help pupils write more vividly; others aim to help students read current or classical literature; and still others attempt to enable pupils to speak more effectively. Practices also vary widely; pupils make lists of new words; they translate one piece of writing into another form; they study synonyms; they look up words in the dictionary; they examine roots; they analyze prefixes and suffixes; they define words; and they list words with a range of meaning — for example, "frigid" to "roasting," and "sopping" to "arid." These practices reveal a deep concern for vocabulary but attest as well to the confusion about how vocabulary can be improved.

There are many reasons for this concern. We are told that vocabulary correlates positively with intelligence; hence we decide that vocabulary should be extended. At the time of our most trusting interest in objective measurement — the 1920's — such recommendations followed the discovery that vocabulary and total scores on intelligence tests agreed closely. We inferred a cause and effect relationship and overlooked the fact that, since both tests involved language, the results would naturally be similar. Nevertheless, the idea persevered, and today many teachers base arguments for teaching vocabulary on the relation it bears to intelligence.

Another reason for stressing vocabulary arises from the observation that many pupils speak and talk without grace, charm, or clarity. They call a hundred things "swell," and fail to make many important distinctions which would be possible through a more discriminating choice of words. Interest in vocabulary building has been aroused also by the common observation that many high school students are unable to comprehend or interpret much that they read. Vocabulary study is sometimes introduced as the solution to this problem. For example, a teacher recently found that his twelfth-grade boys did not know the meaning of the word *appeasement*. He planned a few lessons to teach this word and devised other vocabulary lessons to enable his students to read the news. In a college class reading Robert Frost, fifteen out of fifty pupils could not describe a birch tree; they were not even amused by the statement of one student: "Well, it's a tree something like a pine." It is clear that a few lessons in vocabulary building are insufficient to affect either situation greatly.

How, then, shall we approach this problem, admittedly confused and yet important? Two lines of attack appear feasible: first, to consider what is known about vocabulary (a considerable gain over what was known even ten years ago); and, second, in the light of these facts, to suggest possible procedures to improve vocabulary.

We might begin by noting the word-experiences covered by different vocabularies. These vocabularies include:

1. The words a person uses orally, in one way at least. Tommy says: "I want my ball" (meaning his red-and-white celluloid ball, the only ball he knows).

2. The words a person uses in many senses. Thus one may say: "I am all balled up." "This mud makes a ball on my heels." "This world is but a ball," etc.

3. The words a person can use, perhaps define, but which he employs with little precision. For example, "History teaches us that nations are like human beings, born to die." What is meant by "history"? All the events of the past? Recorded events? Events selected and arranged by certain persons in books? And what do we mean by "nations?"

4. The words one recognizes when he reads them but not when he hears them. A six-year-old child usually has no such words in his vocabulary, but this type of word forms a considerable part of the adult's vocabulary.

5. The words an individual seldom speaks or writes but which he understands when he hears them. "He knows what I mean by *go*," says the proud mother. We

understand many sentences which contain words we cannot define clearly. In this classification there are words from foreign languages. Children whose parents speak a foreign language often understand a large number of such words.

6. The words an individual writes but does not speak. This list grows as the person learns to write freely. Later some of these words may be spoken.

7. The words a person speaks or understands when they are spoken but not when they occur in print. Poor readers encounter many such words.

8. The words an individual uses but which do not occur in tests. These may include slang, profanity, sex words, localisms, etc.

There are undoubtedly other groups of words which will be found in a more comprehensive list. However, the number and complexity of these categories suggest the difficulty students encounter when they seek to estimate vocabulary size. It is therefore not surprising that studies of vocabulary disagree sharply as to size. Let us call attention to the rather remarkable results reported in a recent study and suggest that the reader check them against his own opinions as well as against some other studies with which he may be familiar.

In 1941, Mary Katherine Smith described an investigation of the vocabularies of children in Grades I through XII in two public schools. She attempted to determine "for how many of the words in the test-sampling the child knows some correct meaning." (p.320) *

> Since we were interested in determining the total number of words which had any significant meaning for the child, a broad set of criteria of knowledge was adopted. Thus the child was first given an opportunity to define a word in his own terms, or to illustrate its proper use in a sentence. If he was unable to meet these

---

* M. K. Smith, "Measurement of the Size of General English Vocabulary through the Elementary Grades and High School," *Genetic Psychology Monographs*, XXIV (November, 1941), 313-345.

> criteria he was then given an opportunity to demonstrate his ability to recognize the correct meaning on a four-choice multiple response test. (p.343)

The conclusions of this study lead us to ponder the discrepancy between the vocabularies apparently existing within the minds of children and those included in the rather barren lists found in some preprimers, primers, and reading textbooks.

> For grade one, the average number of basic words known was 16,900, with a range from 5,500 to 32,800. For grade XII, the average number of basic words known was 47,300, with a range from 28,200 to 73,200. (*ibid.*)

"Basic words" are defined as

> those which in the dictionary are printed in heavy type as separate entries along the margin . . . For example, "loyal" is a basic word, "loyalize" and "Loyal Legion" are derived terms. Neither additional meanings for a word nor variant spellings are counted as separate words, but the same stem used in different parts of speech, when listed separately, and compound terms are counted as separate words under such a definition. (p.315)

After considering the varied forms which "vocabulary" may take, and the size of the vocabulary of even the slowest student, one must conclude that many "basal" readers and vocabulary exercises underestimate the child's ability.

It is not, however, the number of words which alone is of importance. Depth of meaning is also significant. For example, two small boys use the word "dog." One means a small, short-haired, friendly terrior; the other a cross, shaggy airedale. Two adults speak of "progressive education." One means a school where responsibility, critical thinking, and honest expression are emphasized; the other thinks of license, lack of plans, and irresponsibility. They argue fruitlessly about being "for" or "against" progressive education.

Thus we see that every individual's vocabulary is extremely complex, not like that of any other human being. It is made up of words he knows in one sense only; those with as many as a dozen meanings; those he can speak or read, or understand when they are spoken, and so forth. Even young children may know thousands of words, a large percentage of which are not to be used in the classroom.

Vocabulary range for a class of English-speaking pupils in the high school is therefore so large as to make futile our selection of a particular list of words for general instruction; the full meaning of many words is so complicated that to teach the various meanings of even a somewhat restricted list is a long-term task. The word "appeasement" used as an example earlier in this paper is a good illustration. In the sentence "Senator X favors appeasement," the meaning culled from Webster — "quieting, calming, soothing, allaying" — would scarcely hint at the association of the word with the international situation. What, then, can we do to help pupils know and use words more effectively?

The following suggestions seem to be logical outcomes of the foregoing considerations

1. We can extend vocabulary by providing a wealth of experience: e.g., trips, hand work, discussion, reading, and so **forth.**

2. We can bring into the classroom more personal writing, and introduce a larger amount of discussion of personal experience. "Free" writing is excellent for this purpose. Informal conversation is valuable also.

3. We can take time to explore the varied meanings of some words. It is natural and normal to hear or use a word in one setting and so to assume that it has only one function or meaning. It will be profitable to examine carefully the varied meanings of certain words and gradually to develop a "conscience" about correct word usage.

4. We can help students to derive meanings from context. Children learn to talk through hearing words in context; mean-

ing is derived from the relationship of the word to the total situation in which it occurs. The student should learn that he should always look to context for meanings. A sound assignment runs something like this: "In this story you will find some new words. Be sure to see whether you can tell what a new word means by studying the rest of the sentence or paragraph. If you cannot discover its meaning, you will want to look up the definitions in the dictionary, and find the one which fits best."

5. We can help students judge the meanings of new words by reference to known words. Advise them sometimes to look carefully at familiar parts of a word and then to guess its meaning. Then they should check the meaning they have derived. Attention to the root, the prefix, or the suffix may help in the case of some words. Study of roots is interesting, and sometimes valuable, but it may prove misleading. We present the root *graph,* for example, and point to some derivatives. *Phonograph,* we indicate, means writing a sound (we have, of course, taught *phone*). But if we do not already know what a phonograph is, we may judge the word to be the name for sheet music (written sounds). *Telephone,* so easily understood as a combination of *sound* and *distance,* might as logically refer to an echo as to a machine on the desk. Thus, in presenting the study of roots, the teacher must safeguard the selection of the correct or applicable meaning from several possibilities. We have spent much time, sometimes with little success, on prefixes. This failure arises perhaps from the fact that the prefixes of many words were integrated and changed in emphasis while they were still used by Romans, long before English was born. Other prefixes were integrated at later times. Thus *con, cum, ir, in,* and so forth, may not be easily separated from the rest of the word. The extent to which time so spent is productive has as yet not been established.

6. We can teach students something about the nature of symbols. We can let them see how abstract or general terms, such as *man, dog, Chinese, poet,* and *war,* cover differences as well as likenesses. Such study will lead students to be cautious

about saying that all poets work by inspiration, all Negroes are carefree, all Russians are communists, or all English persons lack humor. They will say instead, perhaps, that a certain Englishman says this or that, reserving for all Englishmen the generalization that they belong or once belonged to some part of the Empire.

7. We can also indicate that adjectives are words which explain our feelings or evaluations of things—characteristics which are not necessarily inherent in the things themselves. The *bright* boy may seem *very superior* to one person, *average* to another, or *dull* to a third. The *beautiful* girl is so to one, *showy* to another, *pleasing* to a third. Recognition of this fact will lead us to study words as means for expressing unique feelings. Thus emphasis on making descriptions "more vivid" will be employed with great care. For there is no value *per se* in the vivid sentence; the value lies only in the degree to which the expression reveals our feelings or mirrors our experience.

"The artist splashed his colors on the huge canvas," wrote a student. Later, she substituted: "The artist was painting a picture to be hung over our living room fireplace. The face of my mother, almost life-size, pleased me by its likeness to her." Asked about the "huge canvas," she replied: "I have been taught to make things striking."

8. Finally, we can teach pupils that words have more than literal or defined meanings; they carry feeling-overtones which make them rich and beautiful (as in poetry) but often also dangerous and misleading (as in arguments).

If the preceding discussion seems to offer no short cut to vocabulary growth, it is because there is no short cut. Vocabulary is as wide as the experience of the individual and as limited as experience itself. The students referred to earlier in this paper, who did not know what birches were like, could not be blamed; they were city youngsters, aware of a thousand things a Vermont boy might not know. Birches were just one kind of tree unknown to them. They could not be prepared to know the characteristics of different trees without broader experience. Nor could they gain any real appreciation of the birch tree from this poem. By additional reading or through a visit to a park or the woods they might gain the experience required to differentiate this tree from others. Thus this reading activity might properly be regarded as an introductory step in the acquisition of new words. It is essential that the teacher recognize the limitations inherent in certain situations and provide the additional experience essential for building clear concepts of important new words. The teacher who wanted to prepare his students to read the newspapers by giving them the meaning of *appeasement* would have equal obligation to teach many other words connected with political issues. The teacher must learn to select for emphasis those words which have greatest educational value in particular situations. Since there are 750,000 words in English, we cannot hope to teach all the words boys and girls will need. But there are significant and helpful steps we can take in an effort to provide pupils with the vocabulary that best meets their needs; we can also help them to grow independent in developing their own vocabularies. We can encourage the use of words which express what the student knows or has experienced; we can deepen his understanding of the possibilities of expressing shades of meanings through words (poetry is ideal for this); we can open his eyes to simple ways of learning new words (examination of context, and, this failing, recourse to the dictionary, encyclopedia, history, or other reference book); and we can teach him to have respect for the word he speaks and writes. The drive to enlarge his vocabulary will then be his own.

B. INDIVIDUAL EXPRESSION: WRITTEN AND SPOKEN*

Personal, individual, or creative writing is a most important part of a soundly conceived language program. To many persons this form of expression appears merely to be a pleasant pastime,

---

* Paul A. Witty, "Children's Needs — The Basis for Language Programs," in Nellie Appy, (chairman), *Pupils Are People* (New York: Appleton-Century, 1941), Chapter III.

or perhaps a means of release. While these values are important, essential frequently to the mental health of the child or adolescent, there are even more significant outcomes of creative writing. This kind of writing offers a true test of many meanings pupils attach to words.

Clear evidence of one value of creative expression is revealed by the following incident. A few years ago a teacher noticed a small, much-folded piece of yellow paper on her desk. A dandelion had been placed with apparent haste on a corner of the page, which contained the following poem:

> See pure gold?
> Why do people love it so?
> And keep it in a store
> When a yellow dandelion's
> Purer, cheaper — so much more.
> The metal is so hard and cold
> This little weed's a better gold.*

Any teacher might have been pleased by this poem. But in this instance there was unusual delight, for the child who had composed it had been withdrawn, sensitive, and diffident; and this was her first really spontaneous expression. However, it was not her last, for the teacher promptly used the poem as proof of the child's ability. The poem was shared and praised by her classmates, and the incident marked the beginning of a new life for this child — a life of security, self-confidence and successful endeavor. As Natalie Cole states: "Just as we can dig a channel to control the direction of a stream, we can control the direction of our children's activities through praise and recognition."

Other teachers and librarians** have approached this problem in a similar spirit. Their emphasis has been on the value of writing in terms of the child's needs. They have attempted to find out what things different boys and girls want to write about;

---

* To the teachers and pupils of the Willard School, Evanston, Illinois, appreciation is expressed for permission to quote this poem.
** Phyllis Fenner, *Our Library* (New York: John Day and Co., 1942).

then they have tried to provide an atmosphere in which every pupil can write freely and without restriction as to topic or length of composition. Moreover, they have given appropriate recognition and praise for worthy contributions. One of the best examples of a co-operative project in which the teachers of an entire school sought to improve writing is found in *Mental Health in the Classroom.** One finds that creative writing in this school served as an important means of promoting mental health and of fostering the maximum development of boys and girls.

In the examples cited above, the following needs of the child were served: (1) the need for keeping records of significant experience, (2) the need for sharing experience with an interested group, and (3) the need for free individual expression which contributes to mental and physical health.

Many other examples could readily be cited to show how these needs have been met through creative writing. The record of a group of high school pupils who described their reactions during a trip from Holton, Kansas, to St. Louis serves as a good example.** The individual expression varied greatly in literary merit, but the compositions as a group were of undeniably high quality. Another impressive example is found in a book written by the boys and girls of the Ohio State Experimental School. In *Were We Guinea Pigs?* they tell the story of their school life.* Perhaps the most remarkable feature of this book is its clear demonstration of the ability of every child to make a unique contribution to the work of the group. Of course, the writing of the children varied, yet the pieces fitted

---

*Paul A. Witty, (chairman), *Mental Health in the Classroom.* 13th Yearbook of the Department of Supervisors and Directors of Instruction, N.E.A. (Washington, D. C., 1940), Section II. Chapter X by Ethel Cloyd and teachers, Willard School, Evanston, Illinois. See also Paul A. Witty, "Creative Writing Climates," *Childhood Education* (February, 1941), pp. 353-357.

**Nellie Appy, *Pupils Are People* (op.cit.).

*Were We Guinea Pigs? Class of 1938 of the Ohio State Experimental School (New York: Henry Holt and Co., 1938).

together in a pattern that was characterized by unity, coherence, and general excellence.

In the foregoing work, it is abundantly clear that creative writing flourishes when experiences are rich and varied and when unhampered individual expression is encouraged. Again and again, teachers have stressed the significance of increasing the child's sensitivity to the world of things about him if creative work is to reach a high level. And they have been no less insistant on the importance of fostering social sensitivity.

Children's sensitivity to the world of things can be increased by encouraging them to explore their nearby environment, by leading them to visit and observe important local places of significance or interest, and by providing opportunities for new and varied experiences within the school itself. Social sensitivity can be enhanced by offering abundant opportunity for discussion in the classroom. In addition, it is desirable for the teacher to inquire periodically: What opportunities have been offered during the past week for presenting and discussing written work? What experiences need most to be shared? How can every child be given opportunity to share his writing? As such opportunities increase, teachers will find that the mechanics of writing will improve. After all, developing a concern for communication is the surest and most dependable means of engendering a desire to write clearly and correctly.

This emphasis on social sensitivity pays even larger returns. Once aroused, a student's interest in people becomes a dominating concern. Almost every happening is viewed in a new light. Reading, for example, becomes an exploratory experience in which the child feels a vital interest in the problems of the characters. He reads with a new purpose and the process becomes increasingly meaningful. Understanding and retention are at once improved. And, of course, as his experience expands through reading, he accumulates additional vital subject matter for creative writing.

In the following examples, some of the outstanding values of creative writing are illustrated. One of the most important functions is to permit the child to express his reaction to his own experience. The following composition, written by a primary grade child, provides an example of such a reaction:

THE TUGBOAT

"Puff, puff, puff." The tugboat puffs along its way.
It pulls big steamers.
And it pulls barges with coal, bricks, and sand.
And it works so hard.
"Puff, puff, puff," into the dock for the night.

Simple but genuine responses of the type just illustrated take on a more mature form as the child grows older; for example, in this adolescent girl's writing:

> Since I have left home I have seen different things which have reminded me of some of the poetry written by our more modern poets. I have seen people who look as if they were cutting each day to half of its length with sleep's dull knife and I have seen people who give me the impression that the years that are taken off their lives will be taken off the other end. Millay gives these two types of people in her poem *Midnight Oil.*
>
> In travelling through St. Louis, Thursday, I saw several things which put me in mind of poetry written by Sandburg. In travelling through the better districts we passed by streets that were all fenced in. These are known as private streets and the only people using them are those who have their residences on them. The very sight **of them** brought to my mind Sandburg's poem *Fence;* **as a fence they** are a masterpiece, shutting off the rabble, and all vagabonds and hungry men and all wandering children looking for a place to play. The only thing able to pass through the bars and over the steel points are death and the rain and tomorrow.
>
> From these paragraphs one can see that my favorite poetry is that which has to do with our everyday life and happenings, poetry that brings actual daily occurrences into one's mind, such as *Child of the Romans, Clean Curtains,* and *In a Back Alley.*

One finds evidence of the satisfaction derived from creative expression in many situations. The following uncorrected creative response of a hitherto illiterate man is illustrative:

> One beautiful fine day I went fishing in the twilight. The sky was blue and there was a swell breeze blowing. When I came to the lake, the water was calm and clere. I sat down on the edge of a big rock, and through my real, out as far as it would go, and it sunk. I set there for about an hour, and my line started to move. Then I started to real the line in. It wiggled a lot, and I almost lost it. It was about six inches long. It weighed about a pound and a half. That was the first fish I ever did catch. I caught it in Lake Erie.

At first one may be inclined to be amused by examples of this kind — the first creative writing of a mature man. On more sober comtemplation, we look upon these products with humility and with enhanced appreciation — humility over the great satisfaction and real growth made possible in these men through the development and use of a great instrument of education; and appreciation of how basic skills in reading and writing open the doors to a new world of genuine and enduring satisfaction.

Another value of creative writing is found in the way the teacher may come to understand the child's feelings and his needs.* From the long serial story written by a boy and dedicated to "the three dogs I have loved best — one who died, one who was killed, and one I wasn't allowed to keep," a teacher was able to learn a great deal about the way a small boy really feels.

Similarly a child who is unduly embarrassed or worried may reveal and often relieve his feelings in a composition such as the following:

GIRAFFES

If I were a giraffe I would not show myself to the People.
I would be ashamed of myself.

---

* Many examples of children's creative work are assembled in an unpublished doctoral dissertation, by Ethel E. Smith, *Procedures for Encouraging Creative Writing in the Elementary School* (Northwestern University, 1943).

> When I go to the zoo all the people laugh at the
>   giraffes.
> I wouldn't want the people to laugh at me.
> I feel sorry for giraffes.

Sometimes a child's feeling about himself and his own inadequacy is relieved simply by this type of expression:

MONKEYS

> A monkey is so black
> At night I cannot see him,
> But I know a monkey can see
> Such a white-headed me.

We have a glimpse into the mind of the girl who wrote:

> Spring flowers
> You are laughing at me,
> For pop has died.
> No clock stopped when he died
> Only pop;
> I wish it had been me.
> Now you're nodding no,
> And you are right,
> I don't want to die
> For **even pop.**
> Spring flowers
> Stop laughing.

As students grow older their interests and problems reflect increasing maturity and include many significant social issues. These complex problems should be dealt with but they should be treated on the child's level. The teacher should avoid forcing discussion or writing on a level beyond the student's true comprehension. However, there is need for critical examination of current political issues and social problems. The March, 1945, issue of *Educational Leadership,* * now available in a pamphlet, illustrates this need.

We, The Children, published by the Department of Supervision and Curriculum Development, N.E.A., 1201 Sixteenth St., N.W., Washington, D. C. and the Bureau for Intercultural Education, 1697 Broadway, New York, N. Y.

The editors of *Educational Leadership* secured the expression of the attitudes of more than 1,200 students toward race and creed. In these statements one finds illustrations of writing and speaking problems with which a sound language program should deal. In addition, one finds name-calling and generalizations based on one or two cases; careless use of such words as *Negro* and *Jew;* and unfounded rumors presented as fact. It should be borne in mind that these reactions constitute language problems. But teachers sometimes fail to recognize them as such. They correct the child who says *youngness,* and assert that *youth* is the accepted symbol. Is it not as much the teacher's business to inquire into the meaning or the substance as into the form of expression?

It would be well if every teacher of English would read the section in this magazine entitled "Crooked Thinking" (pp.252-256) and consider that these statements were written by American children in American classrooms. It would be interesting to know the proportion of time spent in these classrooms in eliminating errors in usage and putting in commas, as compared with the time devoted to the ideas expressed. What is the important question to ask the child who wrote: *"*I do not like Negroes because they started riot"? Will putting the article *a* before riot correct that sentence?

On the other hand, there are presented in this magazine a number of examples of "Straight Thinking," undoubtedly engendered by teachers who encourage boys and girls to examine basic assumptions and to find out for themselves whether the conclusions of various authors are warranted by their data. For example:

> I feel that it is un-American to have prejudices against any minority group. After all, a prejudice is usually a strong feeling based on what one has heard. I think anyone who has prejudices should look up facts about them. I am sure that he would find that most of what he has heard is untrue. I for a long time had a prejudice against the Negroes. I felt that they were not good. But after reading books and articles about

them, I have changed my mind about them . . . Lately, our class has analyzed some of our prejudices and many of us have found out that they were based on false facts. I wish everyone would do this. I'm sure it would help them a lot.

Exchange of ideas and free communication should be cultiated slowly. We do not burst out suddenly with profound convictions in a group of comparative strangers. The discussion of vital problems develops best in an atmosphere of *wide* exchange, mutual respect, and healthful sincerity. Moreover, the writing program should include many forms of expression — the poem, the humorous sketch, the drama, the short story. Through discussion and exchange of ideas in many fields, human understanding, which is the purpose of language, is gained.

c. Oral Expression and Discussion

Free speech has long been one of the prized possessions of the American people. Nevertheless, we have still to take full advantage of this privilege. Before entering school the ordinary child is said by investigators to use on an average 2,500 different words.* He is, therefore, well prepared to use language as one effective way of establishing himself in his new environment, the school. With him is the group that will for many years be of primary importance to him — his own age group. Beginning with the first day of school he should have an opportunity to talk freely to his companions and to exchange ideas with them. Thus his language will aid him in meeting new problems and in making new social adjustments. Throughout the years of school life the classroom should continue to be a place in which spontaneous discussion and free exchange of experience are encouraged, a place where such exchange is in fact a primary aim. The correction of unapproved usages or of inappropriate expressions is incidental to the larger purpose of cultivating free expression and clear communication.

---

* Some investigators, it has already been noted, would place this average much higher.

There are many obstacles to free exchange of ideas and thought. Religious, economic, social, political, and family backgrounds often interfere. Negro children sometimes hesitate to speak frankly with white boys and girls; some Catholic children are reluctant to talk with Jewish children about certain topics; children of Italian ancestry are frequently hesitant to reveal their use of dialect. In an effort to establish "correct" usage we may easily overemphasize uniformity and lead the child to become self-conscious and unresponsive. In such an event we have sacrificed a major value for a minor gain.

In discussing words, their history, and the way their meanings are changing, the teacher may again capitalize on differences. Those pupils who are accustomed to hearing a foreign language may be encouraged to name cognates or to indicate shifts in meaning. The French boy might be asked to compare the French word *ville* with English words having similar meanings or origin. The German child might indicate what is meant by *Knabe,* and compare this word with *knave*. Or the Russian child might show how his alphabet resembles or differs from other alphabets. Out of differences, strengths are developed, and a healthy respect for individuality transpires.

In every classroom, the teacher will find many opportunities for stressing the meaning and implication of what is said or written. A student recently began a report by stating: "Now that most of our food is going to the armed forces ———." The teacher asked quietly what part of our food is being used by the armed forces. The class discussed the point, produced figures, and as a result the student wrote:

> Supplying food for the several million men in our armed forces has somewhat lowered our share of certain kinds of food. These are———

Careless use of the phrase "most of our food" had led the student into a maze of inconsistencies and a series of unsound conclusions. Discussion and investigation quickly clarified the situation and corrected a language problem.

Does the teacher have the information necessary to correct all the inaccurate statements high school or elementary school children will make? Of course not. The answer to this perplexing problem inheres not so much in correcting children as in helping them to develop a critical attitude toward language expression. The teacher can consistently insist upon the examination of meanings and can see that students explain, interpret, and verify their statements or omit indefensible generalizations. "I just wrote it for English; it doesn't really matter much what I say" represents a situation which should not be allowed to persist.

Many teachers are finding ways to promote critical reading and critical language usage. Sylvia Kay has devised a series of exercises to develop critical thinking through directed reading and discussion in a number of important areas of social understanding.* Selections on topics such as recreation, race, and housing are examined to identify basic assumptions and to reveal conflicting or varying points of view. Students learn to discuss impartially the relative validity of different statements and presentations. Similarly, in a remarkable volume *They See for Themselves,* Spencer Brown relates how groups of high school students have been led to "document" their language usage by experience — by exploration and study of their own environment. In the elementary schools also, one finds teachers seeking clarity by giving special consideration to abstract terms such as *honesty, charity,* and *democracy.* Such words form the "core" of the vocabulary in the social studies. Failure to comprehend the nature and meaning of these words frequently precludes communication, creates confusion, and leads to misunderstanding or actual emotional disturbance.

Some teachers have developed ingenious ways of dealing with these words. Here, for example, is a method employed by one group. The pupils make each week a list of new or confusing

---

* Reported in an unpublished Master's thesis, Northwestern University, 1944. Cf. also Paul A. Witty and D. Kopel, *Reading and the Educative Process* (Boston: Ginn and Co., 1939).

words which they encounter in the social studies. Several words are singled out as being most important for the understanding of the passages under consideration. These words are discussed by the children, who proceed to develop definitions for them. These definitions, at the end of a period of discussion, fall into two classes. The first class includes those words whose meanings, the children agree, are reasonably adequate. In the case of many of these words there are sometimes several equally acceptable and meaningful definitions. These definitions are placed in *Our Social Studies Word Book*. But the meanings and definitions of other words, after considerable discussion, are still not agreed upon as clear and acceptable. Committees are appointed to investigate these words further; they consult various sources for additional relevant information and submit the results of their investigation for discussion at the next class meeting. In this way the meanings of many difficult words are clarified. Teachers are finding that these activities have many far-reaching results, one of which is the development of attitudes of tolerance, mutual concern, and amity. These efforts are indeed reassuring, since part of the battle in achieving success in human relationships is won when language is clear and communication is unimpaired.*

III
CONCLUSION — ENDS AND MEANS

Under its pressure [urge for self-preservation] *so-called "humanity," as the expression of a mixture of stupidity, cowardice, and an imaginary superior intelligence, will melt like snow under the March sun. Mankind has grown strong in eternal struggles and it will only perish through eternal peace.*

                      Adolf Hitler, *Mein Kampf*, 1925 *and* 1927.
                      Page 175 in Alvin Johnson translation, Reynal and Hitchcock, 1940.

---

* Paul A. Witty, "Realms of Gold in Children's Writing," *Elementary English Review* (March, 1945).

The world is concluding an era of horror promised by Hitler in 1925. Can it recover from this tragic epoch? Attention to language will not solve all problems, but an understanding of language and care in its use, in association with other forward-looking movements, may hasten the day when peace, amity, and respect for individuals will prevail throughout the world. It is well to remember that words may be as potent in producing and fostering mistrust and confusion as in leading to understanding and to humanitarian ideals. Two hundred fifty million persons speak English as their native tongue, and many others use it as a second language. This is no tool to be handled lightly; it is indeed a vital factor in developing and preserving civilization.

An understanding of language, suggested in the foregoing chapter, is of particular significance in a democracy. The success of this form of government depends upon the participation of citizens in the choice and retention of leaders and in the development of national and international policies. In order that a democratic form of government may function most effectively, it is necessary that every citizen be prepared to examine conflicting views presented by candidates during election campaigns, and by organizations and legislators from time to time. It was frequently observed that many voters were unable to carry on intelligent discussions during the presidential campaign of 1944. Many of them appeared to be unable to detect misrepresentations or inaccuracies in the presentation of various issues. In the press and over the radio, phrases, sentences, and paragraphs were quoted out of context, with the result that original meanings were altered. Name calling, disguised as classifying, was used by both parties to discredit their opponents. Such distortions of meaning could succeed only with a populace which had not been taught to read, speak, and listen critically.

Meanwhile some teachers continued to present history, English and social studies under a mandate to eliminate "controversial subjects." It is doubtless not the responsibility of these teachers to analyze all social issues. However, unless they can deal with some subjects on which students feel strong disagreement, there is no assurance that their courses will help prepare young men and women to participate intelligently in democratic life. Controversial materials are usually those topics on which the youth of our country need greatest help. One of the most important lessons a pupil can learn is that he can discuss matters of significance without undue emotion or feeling.

The responsibility of English teachers for revealing the role of language in the world today is clear.* Hitler recognized the power of the German language as a force to mold opinion and bind together his people. Russia is uniting her varied peoples by teaching a common tongue. We are beginning to appreciate the significance of Spanish and French in world politics. The use of many languages throughout China is presenting a great obstacle to that country's development. And, within our own country, there are a number of language problems with which students should become familiar.

Many dialects are employed throughout the United States and there are many foreign accents with which the teacher must deal. School programs should respect these variations. The relatively high frequency of the use of dialect to suggest the ludicrous, the association of a foreign accent with ignorance or stupidity, and similar practices reflect the need for more intelligent treatment of language variations. This need will be magnified as the United States expands its role as a world power.

Learning about language without considering the devices by which it is carried is like learning about electricity without discovering any of its uses. Language is conveyed by radio and talking devices, coming to us as pure sound, or in combination with the moving picture. We must teach pupils how to listen to the radio, how to judge the worth of movies, and how to read

---

* Spencer Brown, *They See for Themselves*, Volume III in *Problems of Race and Culture in American Education Series*, sponsored by the Bureau for Intercultural Education (New York: Harper & Brothers, 1945). Cf. also George Salt, *Thinking Together, Promoting Democracy through Discussion* (Chicago: National Council of Teachers of English, Pamphlet No. 6), and Robert H. Thouless, *How to Think Straight* (New York: Simon & Shuster, 1944).

a newspaper with profit. Instruction involving these instruments of communication has frequently been restricted to utilizing them to present or reinforce a minor point. Asked: "Do you utilize motion pictures in teaching drama?", an English teacher replied: "Oh, yes, we have a film of *The Lady of the Lake*." This teacher, like many others, has failed to realize the great potentialities for education through an intelligent use of the motion picture.

Finally, it is fitting to point out that democratic outcomes in the use of language can be achieved only if ends and means are the same throughout the educative process. Roma Gans concluded that one must expect a negligible or zero relationship between the ability to read critically and reading-test scores so long as we fail to give boys and girls experience in examining basic assumptions, and in determining the authenticity and reliability of reports. She warns us of the consequences of this neglect and indicates that high reading ability (as shown by the scores or grades) accompanied by extreme gullibility is an incongruity which a democracy can ill afford to tolerate. Again we recall the words of John Dewey and his concern for democratic outcomes so well expressed in the following:

> If there is one conclusion to which human experience unmistakably points it is that democratic ends demand democratic methods for their realization. . . . Our first defense is to realize that democracy can be served only by the slow day by day adoption and contagious diffusion in every phase of our common life of methods that are identical with the ends to be reached and that recourse to . . . [authoritarian] procedures is a betrayal of human freedom no matter in what guise it presents itself. An American democracy can serve the world only as it demonstrates in the conduct of its own life the efficacy of plural, partial and experimental methods in securing and maintaining an ever-increasing release of the powers of human nature, in service of a freedom which is cooperative and a cooperation which is voluntary. . . .
>
> Only thus can we be sure that we face our problems in detail one by one as they arise, with all the resources

provided by collective intelligence operating in co-operative action. At the end as at the beginning the democratic method is as fundamentally simple and as immensely difficult as is the energetic, unflagging, unceasing creation of an ever-present new road upon which we can walk together.*

SUGGESTED READINGS

1. Boys and Girls Discuss Intercultural Understanding. "Crooked Thinking" and "Straight Thinking" in *Educational Leadership*, II (March, 1945), 252-262. "This is young America speaking. More than 1,200 youngsters, ranging in grade level from early elementary to first year college, contribute their thinking to this issue of *Educational Leadership*."

2. Brown, Spencer. *They See for Themselves*. New York: Harper and Brothers, 1945. The author describes an experiment, sponsored by the Bureau for Intercultural Education and carried out in eleven high schools in New York City and Westchester County. Three documentary plays written by the students are included in this book.

3. Chase, Stuart. *The Tyranny of Words*. New York: Harcourt, Brace and Company, 1938. A pioneer attempt to provide a popular account concerning semantics.

4. Cole, Natalie R. *Arts in the Classroom*. New York: John Day Company, 1940. An unusual account of the creative experiences of young children and their teacher in a Los Angeles public school. Excellent for all persons concerned with guiding reading and language development.

5. Esper, E. A. "Language," in Carl Murchison (Ed.), *A Handbook of Social Psychology*. Worcester: Clark University Press, 1935. Pp. 417-457. Summarizes studies of language development; treats language as a social phenomenon.

6. Fawcett, H. P. *The Nature of Proof*. Thirteenth Yearbook of the National Council of Teachers of Mathematics. New York: Teachers College, Columbia University, 1938. A clear discussion of the relation of language to mathematics.

7. Fries, C. C. *American English Grammar*. New York: D. Appleton-Century, 1940. A study of American English grammar, based on the language of America today.

8. Glasser, E. M. *An Experiment in the Development of Critical Thinking*. New York: Teachers College contribution to *Education*, No. 843, 1941. Some useful suggestions for testing critical reading and thinking.

9. Glicksberg, C. T. "Semantics in the Classroom," *English Journal*, XXXIII (October, 1944), 408-414. Some practical suggestions for improving communication.

---

* John Dewey, *Freedom and Culture* (New York: Putnam, 1939), pp. 175-6.

10. Gray, Wm. S. (Ed.) *Reading in Relation to Experience and Language.* Supplementary Educational Monograph, Number 58, University of Chicago Press, 1944. Compilation of papers presented at the annual conference on reading, 1944.

11. Hayakawa, S. I. *Language in Action.* New York: Harcourt, Brace and Company, 1941. Excellent introduction to semantics.

12. Heyl, Helen Hay (ed.) *English Handbook for Elementary Schools.* University of the State of New York, Bulletin No. 1194. Albany, 1940. Offers practical guidance to teachers on all phases of the language arts.

13. Jersild, A T. "Language Development," in *Child Psychology.* New York: Prentice-Hall, 1941. Chapter V. A comprehensive discussion of language development in the young child.

14. Jespersen, Otto. *Language, Its Nature, Development and Origin.* Henry Holt and Company, 1933. A thorough treatment of the origin and nature of language.

15. Johnson, Wendell. "You Can't Write Writing," *ETC,* I, (August, 1943), 25-32. Suggests a sound orientation for the language teacher.

16. Judd, Charles H. "Language, the Fundamental Institution," in *Psychology of Social Institutions.* New York: Macmillan Company, 1926. Chapter 1. Treatment of the evolution of language as a fundamental social institution.

17. Korzybski, Alfred. *Science and Sanity: An Introduction to Non-Aristotelian Systems and General Semantics.* Lancaster, Pa., and New York: Science Press Printing Company, 1933. An introduction to general semantics.

18. La Brant, Lou. "Relation of Language and Speech Acquisitions to Personality Development," in P. A. Witty and C. Skinner (eds.), *Mental Hygiene in Modern Education.* New York: Farrar and Rinehart, 1939. A brief discussion of the relationship of language to mental health.

19. Marckwardt, A. H., and Walcott, F. G. *Facts About Current English Usage.* New York: D. Appleton-Century, 1938. A good reference book for the teacher who wishes to present a fairly conservative account of modern English usage. Useful to high school students also.

20. McCarthy, D. "Language Development," in Carl Murchison (ed.), *A Handbook of Child Psychology* (rev. ed.). Worcester: Clark University Press, 1933. Summarizes studies on language development.

21. McKee, Paul. *Language in the Elementary School* (rev. ed.) Boston: Houghton-Mifflin Company, 1939. Practical suggestions for developing in language arts in the elementary school in the traditional pattern. 1935.

22. Mearns, Hughes. *Creative Youth.* Garden City, N. Y.: Doubleday Doran, Page and Company, 1937. An important pioneer contribution.

23. Mencken, Henry Louis. *The American Language: An Inquiry into the Development of English in the United States* (4th ed., rev. and enl.). New York: A. A. Knopf, 1936. One of the most significant books dealing with the nature of American English; required reading for all students interested in language development.

24. National Council of Teachers of English. *An Experience Curriculum in English.* English Monograph No. 4 New York: D. Appleton-Century.

25. National Education Association. *Language Arts in the Elementary School.* Twentieth Yearbook, Department of Elementary School Principals. Washington,. D. C.: 1941. Descriptions of school practices in language arts.

26. Ogden, C. K. and I. A. Richards. *The Meaning of Meaning.* New York: Harcourt, Brace and Company (5th ed.), 1938. Thorough treatment of the origin and meaning of language.

27. Ragland, Fannie J. (compiler). *Children Learn to Write.* Pamphlet publication No. 7 of the National Council of Teachers of English, 211 West Sixty-Eighth Street, Chicago 21, Illinois, 1944. Good suggestions for elementary school teachers.

28. Richards, I. A. "Basic English," in *Fortune,* XXIII (June, 1941), 89-94. Presents the thesis that a basic vocabulary of 850 words is sufficient for a practical language of communication. Basic English also has important implications for clearing misunderstandings among English-speaking peoples.

29. ———. *Interpretation in Teaching.* New York: Harcourt, Brace and Company, 1938. Some useful suggestions for teaching are found throughout this book.

30. Roberts, H. de W., W. V. Kaulfers, and G. N. Kefauver. *English for Social Living.* New York: McGraw-Hill, 1943. A report of experiments sponsored by the Stanford Language Arts Investigation Committee.

31. Salt, George. *Thinking Together.* Chicago: National Council of Teachers of English, 1944. Describes a free writing program based on pupil discussion.

32. Schlauch, Margaret. *The Gift of Tongues.* New York: Modern Age, 1942. Simple readable style applied to a difficult subject.

33. Semmelmeyer, Madeline. "Promoting Readiness for Reading and for Growth in the Interpretation of Meaning," in Wm. S. Gray, (ed.), *Reading and Pupil Development,* Supplementary Ed. Monograph, No. 51. Chicago: University of Chicago Press, 1940. Pp. 56-63. Account of an experiment involving application of general semantics to a program of reading readiness. Has important implications for language as well as for reading. Includes descriptions of specific procedures.

34. Treut et al. *They All Want to Write.* New York: Bobbs-Merrill Company, 1939. Entertaining account of the procedures of four classroom teachers who guided the creative writing of children in the first four grades of an elementary school. Stresses individual differences in growth.

35. Walpole, Hugh R. *Semantics.* New York: W. W. Norton and Company, 1941. A simple, direct statement of the meaning of the science of semantics.

36. Witty, P. A. "Children's Needs—The Basis for Language Programs," in Nellie Appy (chm.), *Pupils Are People.* Report of Committee on Individual Differences, National Council of Teachers of English. New York: D. Appleton-Century, 1941. Chapter III. Treatment of children's needs with special application to creative writing.

CPSIA information can be obtained
at www.ICGtesting.com
Printed in the USA
LVHW081309250319
611734LV00020B/644/P

9 780243 486182